Will You

Risk It?

If you wouldn't gamble your savings in a slot machine why invest them in AI?

By

Denis Compton

You wouldn't walk into a casino, tip your life savings into a slot machine and hope for the best.

Yet many hand their money to AI platforms and do exactly that – only with better lighting and fewer flashing lights

Copyright Page

This book is provided for general information only and does not constitute financial advice. Readers should seek personalised, regulated advice before making any financial decisions. Past performance is not indicative of future results. Investments can go down as well as up, and you may get back less than you invest.

Paperback

ISBN: 978-1-918039-52-8

Good Reach *Publishing*

Dedication

To the financial advisers who do an undervalued job in a demanding profession — a profession the public often fails to truly understand. We care deeply, we carry enormous responsibility, and we work diligently to protect the futures of those who trust us. Our fees are our client's insurance policy.

"AI will replace financial advisers."

It sounds dramatic. It captures attention. But it completely misunderstands the true purpose of financial advice.

Table of Contents

Introduction

The Biggest Financial Gamble of a Generation

Imagine walking into a casino. The lights are flashing, the music is thumping, and a thousand machines are calling you with the same silent promise: This could change your life. You sit down at a slot machine. You pull the lever. With every spin, your future hangs in the balance.

Now picture this: you're not in a casino. You're in your kitchen, holding a cup of tea. But you are making the same kind of decision — except this time, the stakes are much higher. Instead of a few pounds on a machine, it's your life savings, your pension, your financial future. And instead of pulling a physical lever, you are clicking '**Invest now**' on an AI-powered platform that promises low fees, automated trading, and the illusion of certainty.

Would you knowingly gamble your future on something you don't control — and don't understand?

Most people would say no. And yet hundreds of thousands are doing exactly that — every single day.

We've entered a dangerous moment in history. Technology has become so clever, so persuasive, so brilliantly designed that it can make us forget we're taking a risk at all. AI-driven investment platforms — marketed as "*smart,*" "*efficient*," and "*the future*" — now hold billions in client assets. They ask you a few questions. They produce a neat-looking pie chart. They give you a number — a "*risk score*" — and tell you everything will be fine.

But here's the truth no one is telling you:

AI can process data. It cannot understand consequences.

It doesn't know your retirement dreams.

It doesn't sense your anxiety when markets fall.

It doesn't care if your spouse falls ill, your business fails, or you suddenly need to support your children.

It cannot look you in the eye and say, "*its okay. We planned for this.*"

For all its intelligence, AI cannot take responsibility. It cannot be regulated in the same way as a human adviser is. It cannot be held accountable if something goes wrong. If an AI platform loses your money, it does not lose sleep. It does not face the regulator. It does not attend your funeral when financial stress shortens your life by ten years. It simply recalculates its algorithms — and moves on to the next customer.

The Illusion of Certainty

AI platforms market themselves brilliantly. They claim to remove human error. They show back-tested charts that only ever seem to go up. They promise discipline, logic, and the removal of emotion — while quietly ignoring that emotion is the number one reason people seek financial advice in the first place.

Because investing isn't just numbers on a page.

It's about security.

Family.

Dignity.

The difference between worrying for years… and sleeping peacefully at night.

AI platforms are designed to "**manage portfolios.**"

Advisers are designed to protect lives.

A Question Every Investor Must Answer

When everything is going well, AI can appear clever — sometimes even unbeatable. But anyone can look smart in a rising market. The real test is what happens when things go wrong.

When the markets crash…

When the government announces a last-minute tax change…

When a loved one dies…

When cash flow becomes tight…

When you panic at 2 a.m. and need to speak to someone who knows you…

Who do you turn to?

Do you rely on an algorithm that says:

"*Market conditions are volatile. Please check our FAQ section.*"

Or do you turn to a real person who understands your situation, who has walked clients through crises for decades, and whose job is not just to invest money — but to protect you?

The Truth You Won't Hear from AI Firms

AI is not the future of advice.

AI is the future of administration.

There is a difference.

Technology can help with efficiency.

It can support research.

It can reduce paperwork.

But when it comes to your life savings — your one chance to build a retirement, a legacy, a future — handing control to an algorithm is not innovation.

It is abdication.

That is the gamble this book exposes.

What This Book Will Show You

Over the next chapters, I will show you:

- Why AI platforms cannot replace human judgement
- The behavioural traps that cause investors to lose money — not because of the market, but because of their reactions to it
- A real example of how bad outcomes can occur when there is no adviser involved
- The regulatory reality — what AI platforms don't tell you in the small print

- The truth about adviser fees — and why they may be the best-value financial protection you will ever buy
- The reality that financial advice is not about investments — it is about your life, your family, and your future.

This Isn't a Book About Technology Being Bad

It's a book about what technology cannot do — and why your financial future is too important to leave to chance, automation, or marketing hype.

So, ask yourself the question that this title demands of you:

Will You Risk It?

Because the future will soon divide people into two groups:

- Those who trusted the machine
- And those who trusted sense, wisdom, and experience — and a human

Which side will you be on?

Chapter 1:

The Illusion of Intelligence

Why AI Isn't Actually Advising You

For the first time in history, thousands — even millions — of people are handing control of their life savings to something that is not alive: an algorithm.

Not a person.

Not a firm with a face and a name.

Not an adviser who knows their children's names or understands their fears when the markets fall.

Instead, decisions once shaped by conversation, empathy, and experience are now being delegated to code.

But here is the truth nobody is telling you:

Most AI investing platforms are not actually giving you regulated financial advice.

They cannot. Legally, they are not allowed to.

They provide guidance, not advice.

And the difference is not minor — it is everything.

Guidance vs Advice – The Most Important Distinction You Were Never Told

In UK financial regulation, there is a clear and critical difference between guidance and regulated advice:

Guidance (AI / Online Platforms)	**Regulated Financial Advice (Human Adviser)**
Generic suggestions	Personalised recommendations
No duty to act in your best interests	Legally bound to act in your best interests
You hold full responsibility	Adviser holds legal accountability
No professional indemnity insurance	Adviser must carry insurance and answer to the FCA
One-size-fits-all	Tailored to your life and goals

Most AI platforms operate in the guidance category — even when their marketing implies otherwise. They use language like *"your personalised plan"*, but in the small print you will always find a disclaimer:

"This does not constitute financial advice."

Because if they were actually advising you, they would be legally responsible for your financial outcome. And that is a responsibility no algorithm will ever accept.

The Risk Transfer Trick

AI platforms appear helpful, but they are designed around one fundamental principle:

Remove liability from the provider and place it entirely on you.

They achieve this through three mechanisms:

1. **Language That Sounds Personal — But Isn't**

   Terms like *"We've selected a portfolio for you"* or *"Based on your profile"* suggest tailored advice, when in fact you are simply being placed into a pre-set model.

2. **Automated Disclaimers**
   When markets fall, the platform tells you:
   "Remember, investments can go down as well as up."
   That's not advice — that's absolution.

3. **No legal Accountability**

   If your portfolio proves unsuitable for your actual circumstances, you cannot claim against the platform. Their defence is simple:

   "We did not advise you. You chose this."

Why This Matters

When you receive **regulated financial advice**:

- The adviser must prove suitability.
- They must document your full personal situation.
- They must show why their recommendation is in your best interests.
- If they get it wrong, you are protected — financially and legally.

When you use an **AI platform**:

- You complete a questionnaire.
- You are assigned a portfolio.
- If it goes wrong, you carry 100% of the risk.

The platform protects itself.

The adviser protects you.

Data Isn't the Same as Understanding

AI can analyse data.

It can run simulations.

It can allocate according to pre-determined models.

But AI cannot understand your life.

It cannot anticipate that:

- Your health might change.
- Your children might need financial support.
- You might be considering early retirement.
- You might want to plan for inheritance tax or future care costs.

AI makes decisions based on inputs.

A financial adviser makes decisions based on insight.

A Tale of Two Investors

Let's imagine two people: James and Helen. Both are 57. Both have £300,000 invested. Both use the same AI platform and answer the same questionnaire.

- James plans to work for another 10 years, has no debt, and is comfortable with volatility.
- Helen has been made redundant unexpectedly and may need to draw income within the year.

The AI assigns them the same portfolio.

Why? Because the AI cannot see context. It only sees data.

A human financial adviser would treat James and Helen entirely differently because

- James needs growth for long-term retirement.
- Helen needs capital preservation and an income strategy.

Same numbers. Different lives.

AI doesn't know the difference.

Advisers do.

The Dangerous Comfort of Automation

AI platforms are designed to make you feel as though everything is under control. The dashboards are clean. The charts are reassuring. The messaging is calm.

But reassurance is not the same as protection.

- An AI platform will let you make a mistake.
- It will not stop you from acting on fear.
- It will not warn you when legislation changes, and your pension is suddenly at risk.
- It will not help your family when you're gone.

It has no duty to care.

Your adviser does.

In the next chapter, you will see what really happens when markets fall — and why AI reacts, while advisers protect.

Because the issue isn't what AI does during good times.

It's what it can't do during bad times.

Chapter 2:

When the Markets Crash Algorithms Panic Too

There's a saying among seasoned investors:

"When the tide goes out, you discover who's been swimming without trunks."

In rising markets, everything looks clever. Every platform, every portfolio, every algorithm appears intelligent and effective —because the conditions are favourable.

A rising market forgives bad decisions.

It flatters weak strategies.

It makes automation look like genius.

But markets do not rise forever.

It's when markets fall — when panic sets in and uncertainty takes over — that the truth is revealed.

And here lies one of the most important truths of modern investing:

AI does not protect you in a crisis. It reacts to the crisis.

A human adviser prepares you *before* it arrives.

The Myth of Rational Reactions

AI platforms are built on a few dangerous assumptions:

- That markets behave rationally over time.
- That investors behave rationally at all times.
- That if your portfolio falls temporarily, you'll stay invested because you "understand the long-term plan."

These assumptions are completely disconnected from reality.

Investors are *not* rational in times of stress.

When your pension drops by £10,000 in a month, your instincts don't say, *"Remain calm — this is a buying opportunity."*

They say, *"Get out now, before it gets worse."*

AI doesn't know your emotional state. It can't hear the panic. It can't intervene.

A financial adviser can — and does.

The COVID Crash: A Real-Time Stress Test

In March 2020, global markets fell by more than 30 per cent in just sixteen days.

It was one of the fastest declines in financial history.

AI platforms responded by automatically shifting portfolios into cash or defensive positions — because the data told them to avoid further loss.

But when markets recovered only weeks later, investors who followed AI's instructions had already locked in their losses. They missed the rebound.

Meanwhile, advisers were on the phone:

"Don't panic. We built your plan to withstand volatility. This is temporary. Stay the course."

Those clients didn't just recover — they profited.

One system followed fear.

The other followed wisdom.

AI Is Reactive — Advisers Are Proactive

AI can only respond to what has *already* happened.

It has no judgement, no foresight.

It doesn't ask, *"Is this decline temporary? Is this panic or a fundamental shift?"*

It simply follows a formula.

Advisers don't just manage portfolios.

They manage *context.*

They understand:

- Market history
- Investor behaviour
- Economic patterns
- Political reality

- Human psychology

They know when to act, when to wait, and when to do nothing.

Experience You Cannot Automate

Experienced advisers have lived through multiple crises:

- The dot-com crash (2000)
- The global financial crisis (2008)
- The COVID crash (2020)
- The LDI (Liability-Driven Investment) pension crisis (2022)

They've seen what panic selling does to a retirement plan.

They've seen fortunes lost — not because markets fell, but because people made the wrong move at the wrong time.

AI only sees data.

Advisers see the danger.

When You're Alone, You're More Likely to Make Poor Decisions

AI platforms rely on one fragile assumption:

You won't panic.

But the moment you *do* panic, the platform becomes a facilitator of your mistake.

It allows you to press the button.

It might even send you a polite message:

"We're sorry to see you go. You can re-enter the market anytime."

When clients try to sell everything during a crash, advisers don't say, *"Click here."*

They say, *"Let's talk."*

That conversation — the one that stops you crystallising losses — is where the true value of advice is measured.

The Cost of One Wrong Decision

One emotional reaction can erase a lifetime of good ones.

- Sell at the bottom of the market — you may never recover.
- Move to cash too early — inflation erodes your future income.
- Withdraw pension funds inefficiently — you trigger unnecessary tax.
- Delay re-entering the market — you miss the rebound entirely.

The cost of these mistakes is far greater than any adviser's fee.

In fact, many advisers earn their entire annual fee simply by preventing one poor decision during a period of market turbulence.

AI Gives You Data. Advisers Give You Direction.

During calm conditions, AI may appear efficient.

During storms, AI merely reports what's happening.

But you don't need *information* in a crisis.

You need *leadership.*

In the next chapter, we'll uncover the foundational pillar of real financial safety: accountability — and why no algorithm will ever sit across the table from you and promise to stand by you, legally and personally, for life.

Chapter 3:

Trust, Accountability, and the One Thing AI Can Never Offer

When it comes to your life savings, there is one question more important than any other:

Who is responsible for the outcome?

- With a human financial adviser, the answer is clear:
- They are regulated.
- They are legally accountable
- They are personally responsible for the advice they give you.
- They must justify every recommendation and ensure it is suitable for your circumstances.
- If they get it wrong, you have protection through systems such as the

Financial Ombudsman Service and the Financial Services

Compensation Scheme (FSCS).

With an AI platform, the answer is equally clear—but far more dangerous:

- It is not advising you.
- It is not responsible for the outcome.

- You are.

The Accountability Gap

AI platforms position themselves with extraordinary care. Their marketing speaks the reassuring language of advice:

"Your personalised investment plan."

"Designed around your goals."

"Smart portfolios tailored to you."

But hidden in the small print lies a single sentence that changes everything:

"This does not constitute financial advice."

That sentence is no accident. It is the legal shield that removes all responsibility from the platform and places it squarely on you.

If your investments fail — that's your problem, not theirs.

If the portfolio was unsuitable for your real-life circumstances, there is no comeback.

If an AI platform's suggestion leads to financial harm, you have no route to compensation.

In short: you are buying a tool, not advice.

Real Advisers Carry Real Risk

A regulated financial adviser is bound by strict legal and professional duties, including:

Fiduciary responsibility — to act in your best interests at all times.

Regulatory oversight — every recommendation must be suitable, documented, and justified.

Professional indemnity insurance — protection for clients if poor or unsuitable advice causes loss.

Legal liability — advisers can be held accountable for the consequences of their advice.

AI carries none of these burdens.

Humans do.

And that is why human advice matters — because someone is truly standing behind you.

The Adviser's Name is on the Line — Literally

When a financial adviser signs off a recommendation, their name is attached to it. Their reputation, their licence, and their livelihood are all at stake. They have a vested interest in your success.

AI platforms do not.

An adviser is incentivised to build a long-term relationship founded on trust. An AI platform is incentivised to scale rapidly and reduce operational costs.

Trust built on profit is transactional. Trust built on accountability is personal.

Responsibility Cannot Be Automated

True responsibility requires:

- Judgement
- Ethics
- Human understanding
- Legal accountability

An algorithm cannot assume responsibility because an algorithm cannot be held accountable.

It has no duty of care.

It cannot be sued.

It cannot be struck off.

It cannot sit before a regulator and justify its actions.

AI is not designed to protect you.

It is designed to service you at scale, at speed, and at minimal cost, without liability.

When Things Go Wrong

Imagine two investors, both suffer losses due to unsuitable investment strategies.

Investor A worked with a regulated financial adviser. They can file a complaint, seek restitution, and potentially recover losses through the appropriate compensation schemes.

Investor B used an AI platform. They are referred back to their terms and conditions — which state they chose the investment themselves and accepted the risk.

Both suffered loss.

Only one was protected.

Trust Is Built on Consequences

The difference between trusting a professional and trusting a platform is simple:

- When a professional makes a mistake, there are consequences for them.
- When a platform fails, there are consequences only for you. That is the true meaning of accountability.

In the next chapter, we will explore the greatest destroyer of wealth — not market volatility, but investor behaviour — and why managing emotion is one of the most valuable services an adviser provides (and one that AI will never replicate).

Chapter 4:

The Behaviour Trap: Why Investors Don't Lose to Markets

There is a myth often repeated in financial headlines:

"Investors lose money because the markets fall."

That is not true.

Investors lose money because they react emotionally when markets fall.

The greatest threat to your financial future is not a bad day on the stock market — it is the decisions you make under emotional stress.

And that is where AI platforms are at their weakest, and human advisers at their strongest.

The Behaviour Gap

Decades of research in behavioural finance have made one fact abundantly clear:

- The average investor significantly underperforms the market — not because the market failed them, but because they failed themselves.
- They sell when they feel scared.
- They buy when they feel confident.
- They act in direct opposition to what creates long-term wealth.

This difference between investment returns and investor returns is known as *the behaviour gap* — the financial penalty of emotion-driven decisions.

AI Cannot Protect You from Yourself

AI executes your instructions.

It does not challenge your thinking.

It does not ask why you are selling.

It cannot say, *"Stop. This decision will cost you years of your life."*

A financial adviser can — and very often does.

The Real Role of an Adviser: Protecting You from Emotional Mistakes

Investors rarely panic because of numbers.

They panic because of feelings.

- Fear of loss
- Regret
- Anxiety about the future
- Headlines that trigger uncertainty

When these emotions rise, people make impulsive decisions that can permanently damage their financial position.

Advisers do not merely manage portfolios — they manage behaviour.

They are there to:

- Prevent panic selling
- Maintain discipline
- Reinforce long-term perspective
- Remind you of your goals and the plan designed to achieve them

AI Speeds Up Emotional Decisions

AI platforms make it dangerously easy to act on impulse. With one tap:

- You can liquidate your portfolio.
- Withdraw at the worst possible moment.
- Lock in losses that may take years to recover.

AI is not designed to stop you — it is designed to facilitate transactions.

A financial adviser, by contrast, is trained to prevent rash decisions and to protect you from long-term harm.

The Cost of One Emotional Mistake

Consider this simple truth:

A 30% market fall is temporary.

Selling during that fall makes it permanent.

Human advisers understand that the worst time to abandon a plan is during a storm. That is why advisers are often the difference between financial ruin and full recovery.

Two Investors – Two Outcomes

Let's take Emma and David.

- Both invested £400,000 before a market downturn.
- Emma works with a human adviser. David uses an AI platform.

When markets fall:

- David panics, sells, and moves to cash. *Losses locked in: –22%.*
- Emma speaks to her adviser, stays invested, and follows the plan.
- Within 18 months, her portfolio not only recovers — it grows beyond its previous high.

One investor paid an adviser's fee — and secured her future.

The other paid almost nothing — and lost his retirement.

This Is Why Adviser Fees Are Worth Every Penny

Protection from behavioural mistakes is not a vague or sentimental benefit.

It is measurable.

It is tangible.

And it is often worth far more than any adviser fee.

A great adviser can earn their entire year's fee in a single phone call — the one that stops you from making a lifetime mistake.

In the next chapter, we will explore why real life is too complex for AI to understand — and why a portfolio is meaningless without a personalised financial plan that evolves with your life.

Chapter 5:

Life Isn't a Formula
Why AI Can't Handle Real World Complexity

Financial decisions are rarely linear.

They do not follow neat formulas or predictable timelines.

They are shaped by life events — messy, emotional, and unpredictable moments that never fit neatly into the limited options of an AI questionnaire.

Yet AI platforms ask a handful of questions and assume your life will follow a straight path.

It won't.

Life changes.

Priorities shift.

Circumstances evolve.

And when they do, a static algorithm cannot adapt — not in time, and not in context.

A Drop-Down Box Cannot Capture Your Life Story

Typical AI platform questions include:

- "When do you plan to retire?"
- "What is your tolerance for risk?"
- "What is your investment time horizon?"

These questions assume your life is stable — when in reality:

- You might retire earlier due to redundancy.
- Your health could change unexpectedly.
- You may choose to support children or grandchildren.
- You could inherit money, sell a business, or face a sudden bill.

AI assumes certainty.

Advisers plan for uncertainty.

Real Lives Are Multi-Dimensional

AI treats money as numbers.

A financial adviser understands that money is deeply connected to:

- Family needs
- Personal aspirations
- Health considerations
- Tax obligations
- Emotional wellbeing

A portfolio cannot be truly optimised unless it is aligned with your life — not just your risk profile.

Example: Two Identical Portfolios, Two Very Different Realities

Consider two clients of the same age, with the same savings and identical market exposure.

- Client A is healthy, enjoys their work, and plans to retire at 67.
- Client B has just been diagnosed with a life-changing condition and wishes to retire immediately.

An AI platform will assign them the same investment strategy.

A human adviser will design two entirely different plans — because the outcomes and priorities are completely different.

Tax, Pensions, and Legislation: The Hidden Complexities

Modern financial planning extends far beyond simple investing. It involves:

- Constant changes in pension legislation
- Allowance limits and tapering rules
- Capital gains tax timing
- Inheritance tax planning
- Long-term care funding strategies
- Sequencing risk management

AI does not proactively monitor these risks on your behalf.

A financial adviser does.

And this is why an adviser's fee is not merely justified — it represents exceptional value, given the complexity managed and the protection provided.

Life Is Not Static — Your Plan Shouldn't Be Either

AI platforms expect *you* to inform them when something changes.

Financial advisers, on the other hand, anticipate change.

They:

- Review your situation regularly or at agreed intervals.
- Adapt your plan in advance of legislative updates.
- Integrate pensions, estate planning, and both taxable and tax-free income streams.

You should not need to know which question to ask.

Your adviser should already be asking it — before the need arises.

You Don't Need a Portfolio. You Need a Plan.

AI platforms manage money.

Advisers manage money *and* outcomes.

- One builds an investment allocation.
- The other builds a life strategy.

And that strategy evolves with you — for life.

In the next chapter, we will address the greatest financial misconception of all: that fees are a cost.

In truth, adviser fees are among the most powerful wealth-protection tools you can invest in.

They are not a deduction — they are a shield.

Chapter 6:

The Truth About Fees: Why a Financial Adviser Isn't a Cost

The single greatest misconception in modern finance is the belief that *lower fees mean better value.*

This myth has been reinforced by advertising, media headlines, and tech marketing to the point where many people accept it without question.

But the truth is simple:

Fees are only a problem when there is no value.

An initial advisory fee of 1–3% and an ongoing fee are not costs — they are wealth-protection premiums.

It is the price of avoiding catastrophic mistakes and securing your financial future.

An AI platform may charge less, but it does not offer *advice.*

It is not offering *protection.*

It is not standing between you and financial disaster.

Your adviser is.

The Real Purpose of Fees

You are not paying an adviser to *pick investments.*

You are paying them to:

- Protect you from emotional panic
- Navigate tax complexities
- Optimise pension withdrawals
- Ensure your income lasts for life
- Shield your family from unnecessary inheritance tax
- Adapt your plan as markets, legislation, and your life evolve
- Take responsibility when things go wrong

That is not an optional extra.

That is financial safety.

If You Think Advice Is Expensive, Try Mistakes

One wrong decision can erase decades of savings:

- Taking pension benefits at the wrong time can trigger heavy tax charges or permanently reduce allowances.
- Neglecting inheritance planning could mean losing 40% of your estate to HMRC.
- Panic-selling during a downturn could wipe out your retirement entirely.
- Drawing income in the wrong order could shorten your retirement by a decade.

An AI platform will let these mistakes happen.

A financial adviser is paid to prevent them.

Why 1–3% Is Outstanding Value

When people hear that adviser fees range between 1% and 3%, they often think, *"That sounds like a lot."*

But consider this:

- On a £300,000 portfolio, a 0.5% annual fee equals £1,500.
- If that £1,500 prevents a tax error or panic-driven decision costing £30,000, it has paid for itself tenfold.

Adviser fees are not a drag on returns.

They are what protect your returns from being destroyed.

AI Platforms Sell Cheapness Because They Cannot Sell Value

AI platforms talk endlessly about *cost* — because that's the only thing they can compete on.

They cannot offer:

- Personal accountability
- Tax mitigation
- Behavioural protection
- Bespoke withdrawal strategies
- Lifetime pension planning
- Family protection
- Legacy advice

So, they distract you with a single number: the headline fee.

But paying less for something that doesn't protect you is not *saving.*

It's *exposing.*

What Adviser Fees Really Buy You

When you pay an adviser, you are not paying for access to markets — anyone can access those.

You are paying for:

✅ Peace of mind

✅ A trusted partner in every financial decision

✅ A plan that adapts with your life

✅ Protection from financial ruin

✅ Clarity during uncertainty

✅ A legal duty of care

✅ Accountability and regulation

✅ The assurance that no decision will ever be made in isolation

In other words, you are paying for *financial insurance.*

And like any form of insurance, it looks expensive — until the day you need it.

On that day, it becomes priceless.

One Call That Earns the Fee

Ask any experienced financial adviser and they will tell you:

"I often earn my entire year's fee in one phone call — usually when a client is about to make a life-changing mistake that would cost them far more than my fee ever will."

A great adviser doesn't just add value.

A great adviser *protects* value.

In the next chapter, we will explore what no algorithm can replicate — *human wisdom* — and why judgement, experience, and foresight are not optional extras, but the essential foundations of lasting financial success.

Chapter 7:

Wisdom vs Intelligence: Why Human Judgement Will Always Beat Artificial Logic

Artificial intelligence can scan millions of data points, analyse trends, and build portfolios faster than any human being. Its processing power is extraordinary.

But intelligence is not the same as *wisdom.*

Wisdom is not just the ability to analyse information—it is the ability to interpret it within the context of real life.

It is developed through experience, through navigating crises, through understanding not just what people *should* do with their money, but what they *will* do when faced with stress, opportunity, or uncertainty.

AI has intelligence.

Only humans have wisdom.

And when it comes to protecting your life savings, wisdom will always defeat intelligence without judgement.

Data Predicts the Past, Wisdom Anticipates the Future.

AI makes decisions based on historical performance. It looks backwards in order to project forwards.

A great financial adviser, however, looks at the world as it is today — anticipates what might happen next — and prepares you in advance.

For example:

- AI sees a rising market and suggests staying invested.
- A wise adviser sees early signs of overvaluation, inflation, or political instability and prepares defensive strategies.

AI can process information.

Advisers can interpret consequences.

The Role of Human Judgement

Wisdom allows advisers to:

- Understand when to act — and when to wait
- See danger before it appears in the data
- Balance financial outcomes with emotional realities
- Consider life expectancy, family dynamics, illness, opportunity, and timing

AI will never call you to say,

"This decision may be mathematically optimal — but emotionally destructive."

A real adviser will.

Why Experience Matters More Than Algorithms

Markets are not driven by logic. They are driven by human behaviour—fear, greed, speculation, and panic.

A financial adviser who has lived through events such as:

- The dotcom crash (2000)
- The global financial crisis (2008)
- The COVID crash (2020)

has seen firsthand how people react under pressure —and how quickly wealth can disappear if the wrong decisions are made at the wrong time.

AI does not remember these moments. It does not feel their impact. It simply processes them as data.

A wise adviser never forgets — because experience leaves a mark that data cannot record.

Investment vs Financial Outcome

There is a profound difference between *investment management* and *financial planning.*

- AI manages investments.
- Advisers manage lives.

AI can maximise return.

Advisers maximise certainty.

AI focuses on numbers.

Advisers focus on what those numbers mean — to you, your family, and your future.

Why Judgement Is Your Greatest Asset

When markets fall, AI reacts.

When legislation changes, AI updates *after* the fact.

A human adviser anticipates.

When life throws you a curveball — divorce, illness, inheritance, opportunity — AI waits for you to update

your information.

A human adviser is already thinking about how these events could impact your future.

Wisdom creates foresight.

Foresight builds security.

And security — that's what true advice is all about.

In the next chapter, we turn to the heart of financial planning — not spreadsheets, not projections, but *people.* We explore what clients truly want when they seek financial advice, and why a real human connection is the greatest financial asset you will ever have.

Chapter 8:

What Clients Really Want (Even If They Can't Put It into Words)

When people first speak to a financial adviser, they often say things like:

- "I want my money to grow."
- "I want good returns."
- "I want to make my money work harder."

But those are not the real reasons they are there.

Beneath those phrases lies something far deeper, far more human:

They want peace of mind.

They want security.

They want to stop worrying.

They want to know they are not going to run out of money, make a mistake, or leave their family unprotected.

They are not just seeking investment performance.

They are seeking confidence and clarity.

Money Is Not Just Financial — It's Emotional

AI platforms treat money as numbers on a screen. But to most people, money represents:

- Freedom
- Protection
- Control over one's life
- Safety for one's family
- A legacy for future generations

Money is not just currency. It is security in physical form.

And when that security is in question, people don't want an algorithm.

They want a human being who understands what's at stake.

The Real Job of an Adviser

A financial adviser's true role is not to beat the market. It is to:

- Remove uncertainty
- Provide structure
- Give clarity where there is confusion
- Turn anxiety into confidence
- Transform financial chaos into a calm, clear plan

People don't want charts. They want certainty.

They don't want predictions. They want protection.

When Clients Say "I Want Growth", They Mean "I Want Security"

Most clients don't actually care about beating the market. What they care about is:

- Knowing they can retire when they choose
- Knowing their spouse will be okay if something happens to them
- Knowing their money will last as long as they do
- Knowing their children will be financially protected

No AI platform asks these questions.

No algorithm can interpret your fears or hopes.

A financial adviser does.

AI Offers Convenience. Advisers Offer Confidence.

Convenience is useful — but it does not provide reassurance.

An AI platform may give you a dashboard.

A financial adviser gives you peace of mind.

An AI can show you the numbers.

A financial adviser helps you understand what those numbers mean to your life.

The Emotional Value of Advice

Clients rarely remember the percentage return they achieved in a particular year.

But they always remember:

- The adviser who helped them stay calm during a market crash
- The adviser who protected their inheritance from unnecessary tax
- The adviser who helped them retire early with confidence
- The adviser who supported them after their loved one passed away

These are not financial services.

These are life outcomes.

In the next chapter, we go deeper into the unique value advisers bring — not by focusing on today, but by looking ahead to a future you may not yet see, and protecting you from risks you don't yet know exis

Chapter 9:

The Future You Can't See (But Your Adviser Can)

Most people make financial decisions based on where they are today.

A financial adviser makes decisions based on where you will be tomorrow — and where you could be if something goes wrong.

AI platforms plan for your present circumstances.

Human advisers plan for your future reality.

And this difference is not subtle — it is everything.

You Aren't Just Planning for Today

Your financial plan must answer the questions you haven't even thought about yet:

- What if you retire five years earlier than expected?
- What if legislation changes your pension tax rules overnight?
- What if your health changes and you need access to capital?
- What if your business is sold and you need to mitigate a large tax bill?
- What if you want to leave a financial legacy for your family — but also ensure they can't mismanage it?

AI platforms will not anticipate these possibilities.

A financial adviser will.

Planning Is Not About Predictions — It's About Preparation

Financial planning is not fortune-telling. It is *risk management.*

A financial adviser doesn't claim to know what will happen.

They build strategies that protect you *regardless* of what happens.

- **AI reacts** to events.
- **Advisers prepare** for events.

And **preparation** is the difference between financial resilience and financial ruin.

Short-Term Thinking Creates Long-Term Problems

AI platforms allow you to make decisions based on what feels right today.

They do not challenge your assumptions.

A financial adviser will:

- Show you the long-term implications of today's choices
- Warn you of unintended consequences
- Help you see beyond the immediate moment

Because a financial adviser is not planning for where you stand now — they are planning for:

- The 85-year-old version of you

- Your spouse after you are gone
- Your children who will inherit your estate
- The tax environment may be completely different by the time you retire

Your Plan Must Be Adaptive — Because Life Is Unpredictable

AI platforms require you to manually update your details when something changes.

A financial adviser:

- Reviews your life regularly
- Proactively adjusts strategies
- Anticipates change before you even think to report it

Advisers don't expect life to stay the same.

They expect life to happen — and they build your plan around that reality.

Wealth Is Not a Straight Line – It's a journey

You are not just building wealth for yourself.

You are building security for your family, structure for your retirement, and a legacy for future generations.

That requires foresight, intelligence, experience, and above all — wisdom.

AI does not have foresight.

It has code.

In the next chapter, we turn to the future — not a world without advisers, but one where advisers who use AI outperform everything else. We reveal why the winning model is not AI alone, but AI combined with regulated, accountable human advice

Chapter 10:

The Hybrid Future: Why Advisers Who Use AI Will Beat AI Platforms Every Time

There is a popular myth circulating in the media and

technology world:

"AI will replace financial advisers."

It sounds dramatic. It captures attention. But it completely misunderstands the true purpose of financial advice.

AI will not replace advisers.

AI will replace advisers who fail to evolve.

And advisers who embrace AI will outperform everyone else.

Because the future of financial advice is not about choosing between humans and technology.

It is about combining the strengths of both.

AI Is a Tool. Advisers Are Strategists.

- AI can analyse data quickly.
- AI can automate portfolio management and reporting.
- AI can reduce administrative time and improve efficiency.

But AI cannot:

- Understand emotion
- Navigate tax legislation
- Protect family wealth
- Act under a fiduciary duty to serve your best interests

AI is the engine.

Your adviser is the driver.

The Adviser + AI Model Is the Winning Formula

AI delivers:

✅ Real-time data

✅ Fast analysis

✅ Efficient rebalancing

✅ Cost-effective administration

Advisers deliver:

✅ Strategic planning

✅ Behavioural coaching

✅ Tax and pension structuring

✅ Personal accountability

✅ Long-term relationship and trust

Together, they form a model that is far superior to AI alone or human advisers alone.

AI Without Advice Is Weak

AI has speed. But without human interpretation, it lacks direction.

AI sees volatility.

A human adviser sees opportunity, danger, timing, and personal impact.

AI sees numbers.

Why Pure AI Platforms Are Already Obsolete

AI-only platforms were built during a time when people believed technology alone would replace professional services.

But the wealthiest and most financially successful individuals in Britain do not rely on pure automation. They rely on expert advisers who use technology.

Technology is not replacing advice — it is amplifying it.

The role of the adviser is becoming more essential, not less.

Clients Don't Want a Platform. They Want a Person.

AI firms sell ease and convenience.

But when you are making the biggest financial decisions of your life, you don't want a dashboard — you want a human voice.

You want someone to:

- Call when you feel unsure
- Explain what legislative changes mean for your future
- Plan for care costs
- Protect your family from tax erosion
- Adjust your retirement income
- Keep you on track through behavioural coaching

AI can't do that. Advisers can — and do.

The Future of Advice Is Human-Led and Technology-Powered

Advisers who use AI will:

- Provide faster, more accurate insights
- Have more time to focus on you
- Spend less time on administration and more on strategic planning
- Deliver better outcomes — not because of AI alone, but because of how they use it

AI is a powerful engine.

But without a human at the wheel, it cannot take you to your destination safely.

In the next chapter, we will explore the wider impact of your financial decisions — not just on you, but on the people you love — and why protecting them requires far more than algorithms or automation.

Chapter 11:

Your Money Doesn't Just Affect You It Affects Everyone You Love

Most people begin their financial journey focused on themselves — on their retirement, their savings, their future income.

But as wealth grows, a deeper truth becomes clear:

Financial planning is not just about you.

It is about everyone who relies on you — today and in the future.

Your financial decisions determine:

- Whether your partner or spouse can live comfortably if you pass away first
- Whether your children or grandchildren inherit a gift or a tax bill
- Whether your family's wealth is preserved or lost
- Whether your legacy is one of security — or of confusion and conflict

AI platforms cannot navigate these questions.

A financial adviser is built around them.

The Hidden Beneficiary of Poor Planning: The Taxman

Many people assume their wealth will automatically pass to their family.

It won't — unless it is structured correctly.

Without proper planning:

- Up to 40% of your estate could be lost to inheritance tax
- Your pension could be taxed unnecessarily
- Your spouse could be left financially vulnerable
- Family members might be forced to sell assets at the wrong time simply to meet tax obligations

AI platforms do not advise on inheritance strategies.

Advisers do.

They ensure your wealth goes where you want it — not where the government defaults it

Your Family Needs Protection, Not Assumptions

Consider this scenario:

You pass away. Your spouse inherits your pension and investments.

But because no estate planning was done, they:

- Pay unnecessary tax
- Lose valuable allowances
- Become overwhelmed by administration
- Do not know how to maintain income sustainably

AI does not step in.

A financial adviser already has a continuity plan in place.

Your plan should not die when you do.

It should activate when you do.

Money Can Unite Families — or Divide Them

Financial planning is not just about numbers — it is about relationships.

Without planning:

- Children may disagree over assets
- Wealth may be distributed in ways you never intended
- Vulnerable family members may be left exposed
- Lifelong legacies can be lost through mismanagement

Advisers understand family dynamics.

They help structure wealth in a way that:

- Supports each family member appropriately
- Reduces the potential for conflict
- Ensures your values are carried forward

AI cannot do this.

It does not understand humans — only data.

Legacy Is Not Built by Accident

You have worked your entire life to build something meaningful.

That effort deserves to be protected and passed on with intention.

A financial adviser ensures that:

- Your spouse is financially secure
- Your children inherit efficiently

- Your wealth is shielded from unnecessary tax
- Your wishes are respected and legally structured

A legacy is not a result of chance.

It is the result of planning.

In the Next Chapter we reveal why — despite the rise of technology — human financial advice is becoming more valuable, not less, and why the greatest danger to your wealth is believing you no longer need it.

Chapter 12:

Why Human Advice Becomes More Valuable in an AI World Not Less

We are living through the most complex financial era in history.

- Tax systems are changing more frequently than ever.
- Pension rules shift with every Budget.
- Investment markets are increasingly volatile, driven by human emotion, geopolitical risk, and speculation.
- Life expectancy is rising, bringing new challenges around long-term care, inflation, and sustainable withdrawals.
- Intergenerational wealth transfer has become a central financial issue for millions.

In this environment, the idea that a low-cost, unregulated AI platform could replace the strategic guidance of an experienced financial adviser isn't just unrealistic—it's dangerous.

Technology is not reducing the need for advice.

It is increasing it.

AI Simplifies Transactions — Not Lives

AI platforms can rebalance a portfolio or execute trades efficiently. That may save time.

But financial advice is not about transactions — it is about outcomes:

- Will your money last as long as you do?
- Will you avoid unnecessary tax?
- Will your spouse be protected?
- Will your wealth pass on as intended?
- Will you avoid catastrophic decisions when markets fall?

These are human issues, not mathematical ones.

Complexity Demands Expertise

The more complex your financial life becomes, the more valuable real advice becomes.

Examples of situations AI cannot navigate include:

- Pension Lifetime Allowance planning and transitional protections
- Money Purchase Annual Allowance restrictions
- Sequencing risk in retirement withdrawals
- Blended tax strategies across pensions, ISAs, and general accounts
- Care funding considerations
- Legacy structuring, trusts, and inheritance tax mitigation

These are not optional extras.

They are central to preserving your wealth over the long term.

An AI platform will never answer these questions —because it cannot even ask them.

Advice Is Not About Beating the Market — It's About Avoiding Ruin

Financial success is not determined by outperforming a benchmark. It is determined by:

- Avoiding major losses
- Staying disciplined
- Navigating tax and legislation
- Protecting family outcomes
- Making the right decisions at the right time

AI may help you access investments.

Only an adviser helps you prevent financial ruin.

This is why adviser fees are not expensive — **they represent exceptional value.**

It is the cost of certainty in an uncertain world.

Human Advice Is the One Advantage You Cannot Automate

AI will continue to improve. It will become faster and more efficient. But it will never:

- Care about your family
- Be personally accountable
- Offer judgement or foresight
- Provide reassurance in times of fear
- Build a relationship with you based on trust

AI may be intelligent, but it will never be responsible.

Your adviser is.

In the Final Chapter we arrive at the ultimate choice — one that defines not just your financial future, but your peace of mind:

Will you risk it?

Final Chapter

The Final Question – Will You Risk It?

You have now seen the truth.

- AI platforms are not financial advisers. They provide access, but not protection.
- Markets don't destroy wealth — panic does.
- Financial outcomes are not determined by products —they are determined by decisions.
- Your money is not just about you — it affects your family, your future, and your legacy.
- The greatest threats to your wealth are hidden in tax rules, legislation, behavioural mistakes, and life's unpredictability.
- And the single most powerful protection you have is not an algorithm — it is a regulated, accountable human adviser working in your best interests.

So now the most important question remains:

Will you risk your life savings on an AI platform that cannot protect you?

Or

Will you choose the safety of real advice — from a real professional who carries real responsibility for your financial future?

The Truth About Fees – One Last Time

If you remember only one message from this book, let it be this:

Adviser fees are not a cost; they are insurance against financial catastrophe.

- They protect you from behavioural mistakes.
- They help you avoid unnecessary tax.
- They provide clarity when life changes.
- They defend your wealth during market crashes.
- They give you access to expertise that prevents lifelong errors.
- They secure the financial future of those you love, long after you are gone.

The real cost is not the fee.

The real cost is what happens if you don't have that protection.

You Only Get One Retirement. One Legacy. One Shot.

AI platforms will not call your spouse when you pass away.

They will not stay up at night thinking about your financial stability.

They will not carry legal accountability for your future.

They will not sit across from your family and guide them with humanity, dignity, and care.

But a financial adviser will.

What Type of Investor Will You Choose to Be?

There are two types of people in the world of investing:

1. Those who trust algorithms with their future, because it feels easy.

They may save a small fee today…

But they leave their wealth vulnerable to every market crash, tax trap, emotional mistake, and life event that they never saw coming.

2. Those who work with a financial adviser who understands their life.

They pay a fee to invest in guidance, in protection, in discipline, in foresight.

And in return, they gain certainty, confidence, security, and control.

Only one of these groups retires with real peace of mind.

The Final Decision Is Yours

This book was not written to entertain you.

It was written to protect you.

You now know the risks.

You now understand the difference between AI platforms and true financial advice.

You now see that adviser fees are not something to be avoided — but something to be gratefully secured.

So, I leave you with the question that will define your financial future:

Will you risk it?

Or will you protect it — with real advice, from a real person, who is truly invested in you?

Bonus Section

10 Questions You Must Ask Before You Trust Anyone with Your Life Savings

If an adviser — or AI platform — cannot confidently answer these questions, you should not trust them with your financial future.

These questions are not just a checklist…

They are your shield against poor advice, hidden risks, and automated systems that carry no accountability.

Use Them. Protect Yourself. Make The Right Choice.

1. Are you personally regulated and legally accountable for the advice you give?

Why it matters: Only FCA-regulated advisers are legally obligated to act in your best interests. AI platforms are not.

✅ What you should hear:

"Yes, I am regulated by the Financial Conduct Authority and fully accountable for the advice I give."

2. If something goes wrong, who is legally responsible — me or you?

Why it matters: With AI platforms, you carry all the risk.

✅ What you should hear:

"I carry full responsibility for the advice. You are protected."

3. How will you protect me from making emotional mistakes when markets fall?

Why it matters: Behavioural mistakes cost more than market downturns.

✅ What you should hear:

"I will coach you through volatility and prevent decisions that could damage your long-term future."

4. Do you help with tax planning, pensions, inheritance, and life protection — or just investments?

Why it matters: Wealth management is about your entire life, not just your portfolio.

✅ What you should hear:

"Yes, I provide full financial planning, not just investment management."

5. What am I paying for, and how does your fee protect me financially?

Why it matters: Fees are only expensive in the absence of value.

✅ What you should hear:

"You are paying for protection, strategy, tax efficiency, behavioural guidance, and security — all of which far exceed the cost of the fee."

6. How often will you review my situation and make adjustments?

Why it matters: Your life changes. Your plan must change with it.

✅ What you should hear:

"We will regularly review your plan and adapt proactively."

7. Who looks after my family if something happens to me?

Why it matters: Financial planning doesn't end with your life.

✅ What you should hear:

"I will help and advise on how to protect your family's financial continuity."

8. Are you independent and able to choose the best options from the entire market?

Why it matters: Restricted advice means limited outcomes.

✅ What you should hear:

"Yes. I act solely in your best interests and have access to the full marketplace."

9. Can you show me how you have helped clients during market crashes or major tax changes?

Why it matters: You are not looking for theory — you are looking for proven protection.

✅ What you should hear:

"Yes. Let me show you real examples."

10. How will you ensure my wealth is passed on efficiently and protected from unnecessary tax?

Why it matters: Without planning, your largest beneficiary could be HMRC.

✅ What you should hear:

"I will create a plan that ensures your wealth goes where you intend — not where the system defaults it."

About the Author

Denis Compton is an experienced Independent Financial Adviser with over 30 years in the profession.

As the founder of Western Financial Planning Ltd, he has helped individuals, families, and business owners — predominantly in the South West of the UK— build, protect, and preserve their wealth through every market cycle and legislative change.

Throughout his career, Denis has guided clients through some of the most turbulent financial periods in modern history, helping them achieve long-term financial security with confidence and peace of mind.

He writes and speaks extensively about the importance of regulated financial advice in an increasingly automated world, consistently promoting the value that professional advisers bring to investors and their families.

Denis believes financial advice is not about chasing returns — it is about protecting futures.

www.ingramcontent.com/pod-product-compliance
Lightning Source LLC
LaVergne TN
LVHW022024200926
848481LV00007B/2531
9781918039528